I "WannaBee"
INTRODUCTION

I am a retired registered nurse who spent the last twenty years of my career as a school nurse. Often when children visited my clinic, as a means of distracting them from their discomfort, I would ask them what they wanted to be when they grew up. For many years I was amused at the various choices. However, over time I began to notice that, far too often, when asked, many of them would just shrug their shoulders and seemed indifferent. I began to worry that some of our children had no goals or aspirations for the future. I decided that this was an issue that needed to be addressed.

Thus we have: **I "WannaBee" Designs** . . . beginning with this Activity and Coloring Book. It offers insight into the definitions of, and some of the requirements for 27 different careers. It provides activities in an interactive and entertaining way. Hopefully it will spark new interests in your children.

I "WannaBee" Designs
Created by Phillis Jones, RN
Illustrations by Hashim Clark

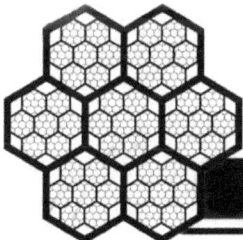

Cover Design by Hashim Clark
Book interior design by Phillis Jones and Hashim Clark
Certificate of Registration Number TXu 2-003-489
issued under the seal of the Copyright Office
in accordance with title 17, United States Code.
under the name of "Wannabee" Careers Coloring and Activity Book

ISBN 978-0-9986664-0-2

Table Of Contents

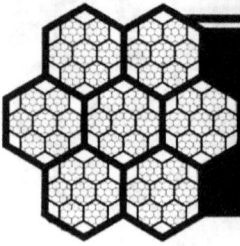

ACCOUNTANT
(ac-count'-ant)

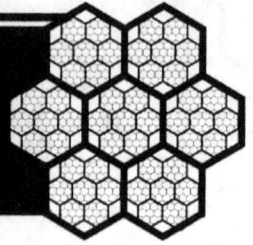

Accountants are people who maintain the records of money that is spent and received by companies and individuals. They work at a desk with computers, calculators and record books.

Use the CLUE BOX to name these "tools of the trade" for an Accountant

_____

_____

CLUE BOX

* books
* calculator
* computer
* desk

_____

_____

(answers on page 57)

QUESTIONS..........................

1. What does an accountant do?

   _____

2. What kinds of tools are used by an accountant?

   _____

3. How does someone become an accountant?

   _____

4. Can you name an accountant (Perhaps a relative or family friend)?

   _____

5. Would you like to become an accountant, and why?

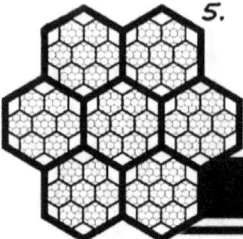

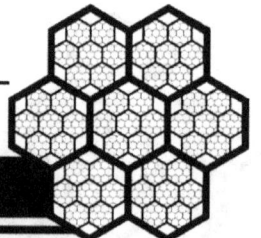

   _____

ACCOUNTANT

I like to add, subtract, divide.
I like what numbers do.
Accountants get to do those things,
and someday I will too.

Write your own poem here

_____
_____
_____
_____

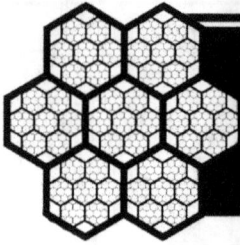
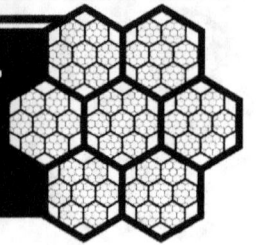

ANTHROPOLOGIST

(an'thro-pol'o-gist)

Anthropologists are people who study humankind. They study human societies and cultures; how societies behaved in the past and how they behave now. Cultures are groups of people who live and work together. Anthropologists study societies and cultures that lived hundreds or thousands of ago. They examine artifacts and bones. Artifacts are objects made by human beings, such as dishes, furniture, buildings, tools and anything made by man. Anthropologists need to earn a college degree.

Use the Clue Box to unscramble the words below each picture.

CLUE BOX

* artwork
* world
* artifact
* mummy tomb
* examine

FACARTIT

_____

WARTORK

_____

MINEXAE

_____

YUMMM MBOT

_____

RLDWO

_____

(answers on page 57)

QUESTIONS

1. What does an anthropologist do?

_____

2. What are ancient cultures?

_____

3. What are artifacts?

_____

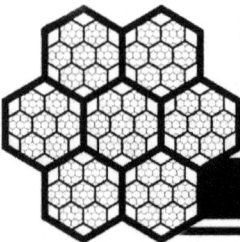
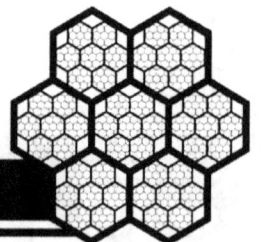

ANTHROPOLOGIST

Anthropologists are people
who observe the life of man;
how different people lived and died,
and how we all began.

Write your own poem here

_____
_____
_____
_____

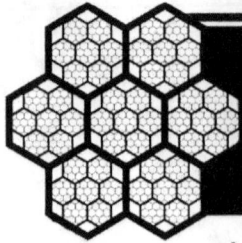 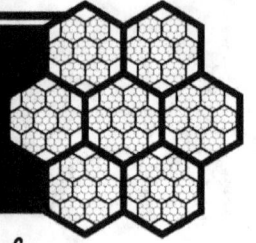

ARCHITECT
(ar'-chi-tect')

Architects are people who design and supervise the construction of buildings, bridges or other structures like the pyramids. They need a college degree. Some of the tools they use are rulers, tape measures, desk, paper, pencils, and calculators to make measurements and create different designs.

Circle the pictures that have something to do with architects.

CLUE BOX

* buildings
* architect tools
* structures like the pyramids
* measuring tape

(answers on page 57)

QUESTIONS ••••••••••••••••••••••••

1. What does an architect do?

_____

2. What are some tools an architect would use?

_____

3. How does someone become an architect?

_____

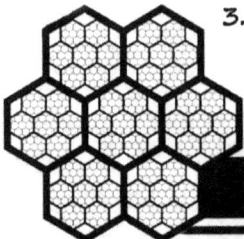

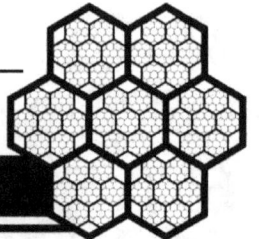

ARCHITECT

I like all kinds of building blocks...
to make things large and small.
Build bridges, homes and churches...
maybe a shopping mall.

Write your own poem here

_____

_____

_____

_____

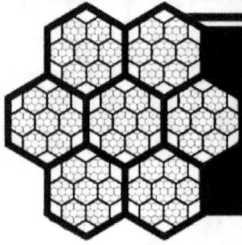
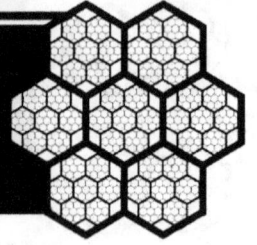

ASTRONAUT
(as'-tro-naut)

An astronaut is someone who is trained to pilot or navigate a spacecraft or, to work as a crew member on that craft. They must have a college education in astrophysics. Astrophysics is the science that deals with stars, planets and galaxies. Some of the tools they use are spaceships, space suits, and special tools designed for use in outer space

Draw a line from the "tools of the trade" to the matching phrase.

STARS

SPACE SUIT

PLANETS

SPACESHIP

(answers on page 57)

QUESTIONS.................................

1. What does an astronaut do?

_____

2. What kinds of tools are used by an astronaut?

_____

3. How does someone become an astronaut?

_____

4. Can you name an astronaut?

_____

5. Would you like to become an astronaut, and why?

_____

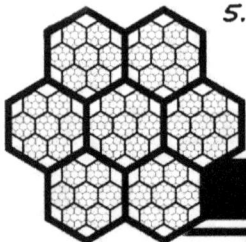
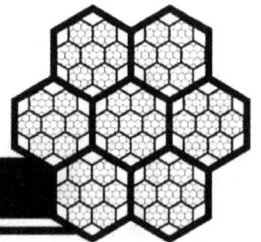

ASTRONAUT

I love what's in the night time sky.
I love the moon and stars.
I want to travel into space
and maybe visit Mars.

Write your own poem here

_____
_____
_____
_____

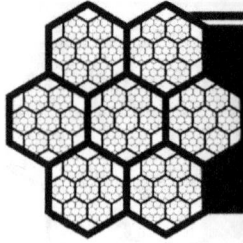
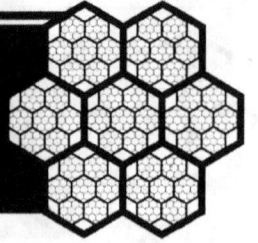

AUDIOLOGIST
(au'di-ol'o-gist)

An audiologist is a doctor who examines ears and tests for hearing problems. Audiologists have a college degree and a Ph.D. (doctorate degree). They work in schools, clinics, and private offices.

CLUE BOX

* audiologist
* audiometer
* ear
* otoscope

Audiometer- used to test hearing in the ear

Otoscope - used to look inside the ear

Ear

Use the CLUE BOX to unscramble the words below to find things related to audiologists

eopotsco   rea   dioauoltisg   audemtioer

_____   ___   _____   _____

(answers on page 58)

QUESTIONS..............................

1. What does an audiologist do?

_____

2. What kinds of tools are used by an audiologist?

_____

3. How does someone become an audiologist ?

_____

4. Can you name an audiologist?

_____

5. Would you like to become an audiologist, and why?

_____

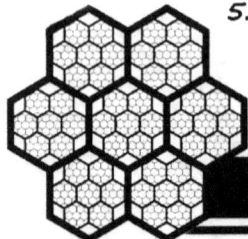
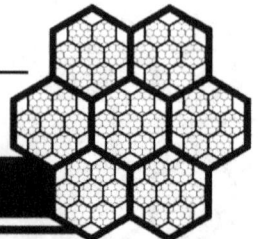

AUDIOLOGIST

Audiologists are doctors
who make sure that you can hear.
They use a special kind of tool
to look inside your ear.

Write your own poem here
_____
_____
_____
_____

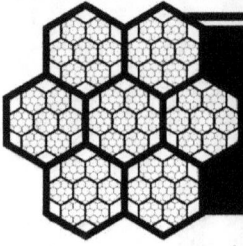
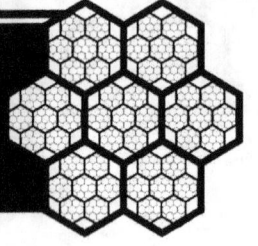

CARPENTER
(car'-pen-ter)

A carpenter is someone who makes, finishes, and repairs wooden objects and structures. To become a carpenter, a person would need to attend a trade school and/or be an apprentice (student of a professional carpenter).

Use the tool box to name the carpenter's tools below.

CLUE BOX
* toolbox
* saw
* hammer
* wrench
* screwdriver

_____ _____ _____ _____

QUESTIONS........................

(answers on page 58)

1. What does an carpenter do?

   _____

2. What kinds of tools are used by a carpenter?

   _____

3. How does someone become an carpenter?

   _____

4. Can you name an carpenter?

   _____

5. Would you like to become an carpenter, and why?

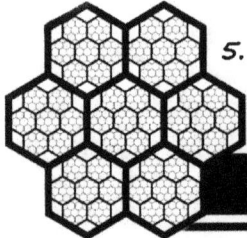
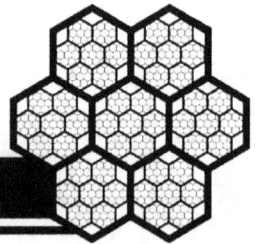

   _____

CARPENTER

Carpenters build everything...
a house and all that's in it.
With special tools and special skills...
I'm sure there is no limit.

Write your own poem here

_____
_____
_____
_____

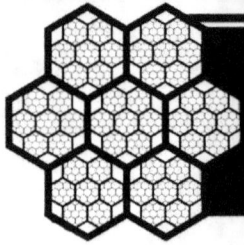

CLERGY PERSON
(cler'gy or cler'ics)

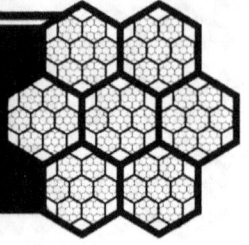

Clergy People (or clerics) are leaders of many different religious groups.
Some different kinds of clergy people (or clerics) are: Ministers, Priests, Rabbis, Imams,
and Monks. They guide their followers in the practices and rules of their religions.
Some of their work places are churches, synagogues, temples, and mosques.

MATCH-UP

Draw a line from the picture to the word that it identifies.

temple   synagogue   church   mosque

(answers on page 58)

QUESTIONS.............................

1. What does a clergy person do?

_____

2. What are some different kinds of clergy leaders?

_____

3. Can you name a clergy leader?

_____

4. Name some clergy workplaces?

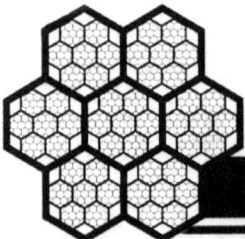

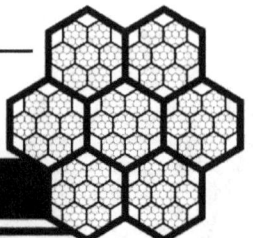

_____

CLERGY

A person of the clergy
has a calling from above.
They help to heal the spirit
and they do it all with love

Write your own poem here

_____
_____
_____
_____

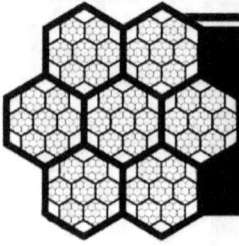

COMPUTER PROGRAMMER
(com-put'-er pro'-gram-mer)

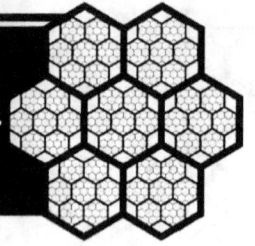

A computer programmer is a person who designs and tests programs for computers. They "trouble shoot" which means they look for problems with computers and solve those problems. They usually have earned a college degree followed by technical certification. In order to get technical certification they must take a test to prove that they understand a specific computer program. They work in offices or any place where there are computers.

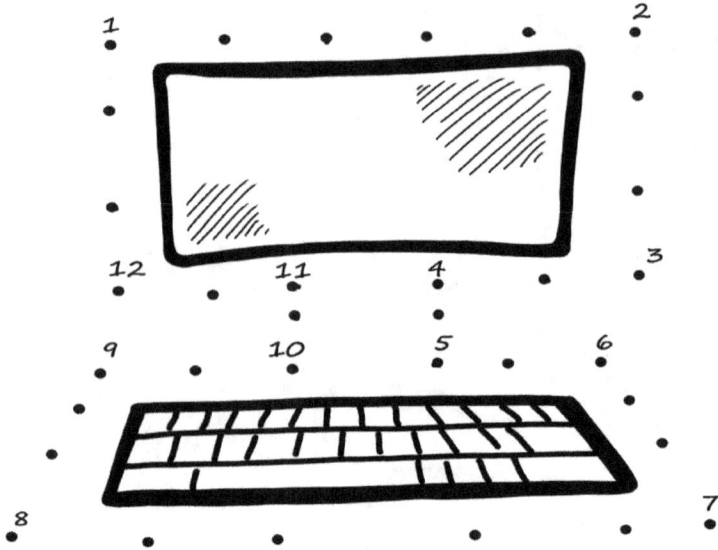

WHAT IS IT?
Connect the dots
from 1 to 12
and back to 1

(answers on page 58)

QUESTIONS.............................

1. What does a computer programmer do?

_____

2. Where do computer programmers work?

_____

3. How does someone become a computer programmer?

_____

4. Do you like math, numbers, puzzles, and solving problems?

_____

5. Would you like to become a computer programmer and why?

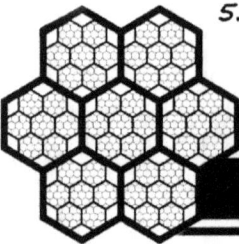

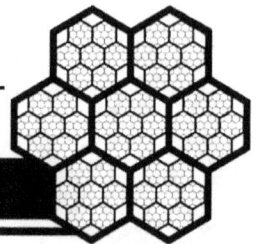

_____

COMPUTER PROGRAMMER

Computers can do anything
we make them do... it's true!
Someday I'll learn the how and why
they do just what they do.

Write your own poem here

_____
_____
_____
_____

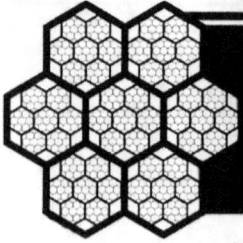

DOCTOR
(doc'-tor)

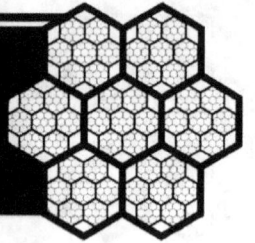

A doctor is someone who is licensed to practice medicine. Doctors have many years of training and a degree from college. After college they must earn a degree from medical school. After finishing medical school they must do an internship, which is like an apprenticeship. An internship is where they practice what they have learned. Some of the many different kinds of doctors are: pediatricians who treat children, surgeons who operate on patients, general practitioners who treat all kinds of patients and cardiologists who treat heart disease.

Draw a line to show the path you need to take to become a Doctor.

COLLEGE

MEDICAL SCHOOL

ELEMENTARY / HIGH SCHOOL

HOSPITAL

(answers on page 59)

QUESTIONS••••••••••••••••••••••••

1. What does it take to become a doctor?

_____

2. What are some different kinds of doctors?

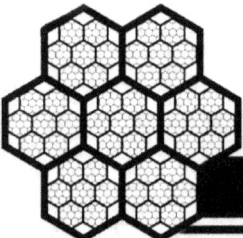

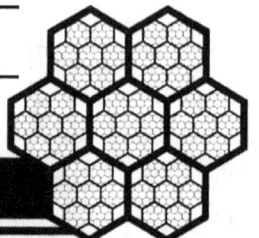

_____

_____

DOCTOR

There are all kinds of doctors
who will treat us when we're ill.
They try to keep us healthy,
Keep us strong and make us well.

Write your own poem here

_____
_____
_____
_____

EMERGENCY MEDICAL TECHNICIAN
EMT
(e-mer'-gen-cy med'-i-cal tech-ni'-cian)

An Emergency Medical Technician (EMT) is someone who has taken
special classes to become certified so he/she can give emergency medical treatment.
They treat sudden illnesses or injuries. They are trained to bandage wounds, give medicine,
deliver babies, help choking or drowning victims and much more. They ride in ambulances so they
can get to patients quickly. Then they give emergency treatment and rush them to a hospital.

Name the EMT "Tools of the Trade"

CLUE BOX
* ambulance
* bandages
* stethoscope
* stretcher
* gloves

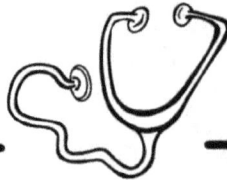

(answers on page 59)

QUESTIONS •

1. What does an EMT (Emergency Medical Technician) do?

_____

2. What do EMTs use to get around?

_____

3. How does someone become an EMT?

_____

4. Would you like to become an EMT, and why?

_____

EMERGENCY MEDICAL TECHNICIAN

Emergency Medical Technician;
that says a lot to me.
They help the sick and injured,
and we call them EMTs.

Write your own poem here

_____
_____
_____
_____

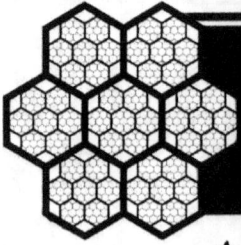
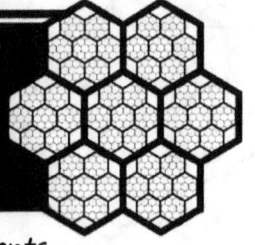

FIREFIGHTER
(fire'fight'-er)

A Firefighter is someone who is trained to fight fires and respond to accidents where a fire may start. Firefighters are trained at special academies (schools). Some are full-time firefighters that sleep in the firehouse when there is no fire alarm. Others are volunteer firefighters who work part-time and come from home or work to respond to fire alarms. They travel in fire trucks with ladders. They wear heavy rain coats and helmets. They use hoses and pickaxes to fight flames. They attach the hoses to fire hydrants which may be the source of water near the fire.

Circle the words that have something to do with being a firefighter.

hose   helmet   banana   hydrant   lollipop   sweater   water

flames   basketball   boots   gorilla   ladder   pickaxes   alarm

Can you draw a picture of a Firefighter?

(answers on page 59)

QUESTIONS ••••••••••••••••••••••

1. Where does a firefighter sleep when he/she is on duty, and there is no fire?

_____

2. What is a volunteer firefighter?

_____

3. What do firefighters do?

_____

4. How does someone become a firefighter?

_____

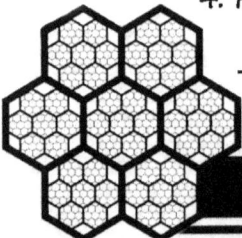
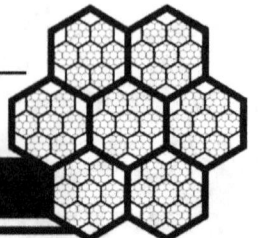

FIREFIGHTER

Firefighters save our homes,
our pets and forests too.
Protect the lives of those we love.
That's what I want to do.

Write your own poem here

_____
_____
_____
_____

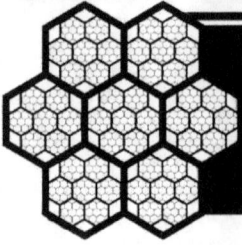
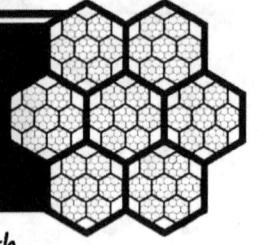

GEOLOGIST
(ge-ol'-o-gist)

A geologist is someone who studies the origin (beginnings) of the earth.
Geologists also study the history and structure of the earth. They dig in caves,
on mountains, in deserts, and all around the world. They are looking for clues that will
tell us how the earth came to be the way it is. Sometimes they find very precious gems.
Sometimes they find gold or silver. Sometimes they find different kinds of ore.
A college degree is needed to become a geologist.

Circle the pictures that have something to do with being a Geologist

(answers on page 59)

QUESTIONS •••••••••••••••••••••••

1. Where do geologist work?

_____

2. What are geologists looking for?

_____

3. How can someone become a geologist?

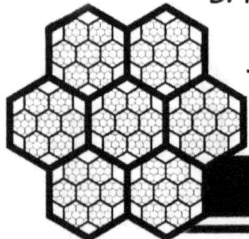
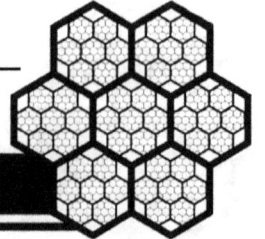

GEOLOGIST

A special type of scientist
will study Earth's time clock.
They dig and probe around the world.
Geologists...THEY ROCK!

Write your own poem here

_____
_____
_____
_____

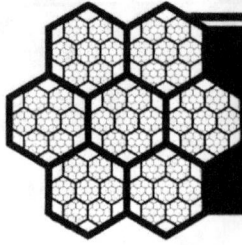

GUIDANCE COUNSELOR
(guid'-ance coun' sel-or)

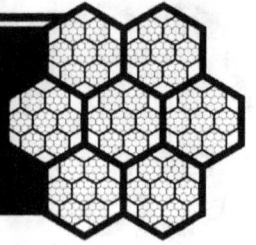

A guidance counselor is someone with a college degree who has taken courses in how to guide and advise students in career and personal matters. They also teach students how to solve social problems and get along with each other.

Below are some of the ways guidance counselors help us. Draw a line from the picture to the phrase that matches.

Prepare us for a higher education

Help us choose the right path

Help us with problem solving

Help us learn how to work together

(answers on page 60)

QUESTIONS ••••••••••••••••••••••••

1. How does someone become a guidance counselor?

_____

2. Where do guidance counselors work?

_____

3. Would you like to become a guidance counselor, and why?

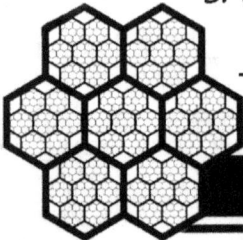

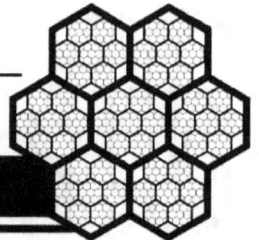

_____

GUIDANCE COUNSELOR

A guidance counselor I will be —
Help students with a plan.
I'll guide them and I'll let them know
just how to say "I can".

Write your own poem here

_____
_____
_____
_____

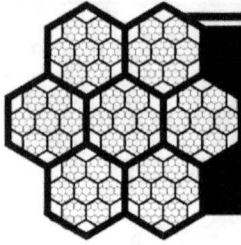
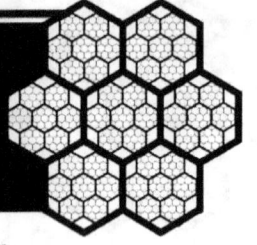

LAWYER
(law'-yer)

A lawyer is someone who is trained and educated to give legal advice.
Lawyers represent clients in court. They must earn a college degree and then attend
law school. After law school, they must pass the Bar Exam which is a test of a person's
knowledge of the law. They work in law offices and court rooms.

Draw a line to show the path to take in order to become a lawyer.

ELEMENTARY SCHOOL

COLLEGE PRE-LAW

HIGH SCHOOL

LAW SCHOOL

PASS THE BAR EXAM

...AND NOW YOU'RE A LAWYER

(answers on page 60)

QUESTIONS •

1. Do you think you have what it takes to be a lawyer?

_____

2. Where do lawyers work?

_____

3. What is the Bar Exam?

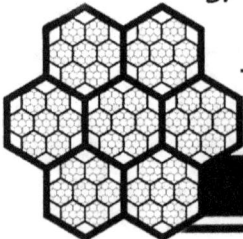
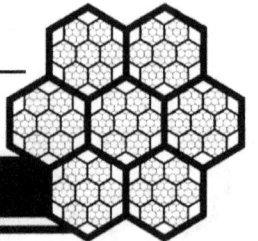

_____

LAWYER

Sometimes Lawyers go to court.
Face a judge and jury too.
They try to prove their cases.
That's just some of
what they do.

Write your own poem here

_____

_____

_____

_____

LIBRARIAN
(li-brar'-i-an)

A librarian is someone with a college degree in library sciences. He or she knows the organization and functioning of a library. Librarians can assist with research and finding the right books for the right projects. They work with all kinds of books, reference materials and computers. "Story time", book clubs, and special interest groups for people of all ages, are just some of the programs that they arrange. There are libraries in schools, public library buildings, offices, and some companies.

Circle the pictures that have something to do with Librarians

(answers on page 60)

QUESTIONS ••••••••••••••••••••••••••••

1. Where are libraries found?

_____

2. How does someone become a librarian?

_____

3. What do librarians do?

_____

LIBRARIAN

A librarian is someone
who will look up things in books.
show us how to do the research;
tell us just where we should look.

Write your own poem here

_____

_____

_____

_____

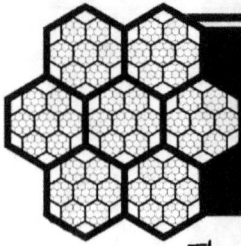
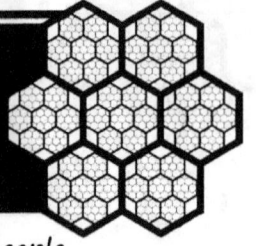

MARINE BIOLOGIST
(mar-ine' bi-ol'-o-gist)

The word marine describes things related to oceans and seas. Biologists are people who study living things and their surroundings. Thus, a marine biologist is someone who explores and treats animal and plant life in oceans and seas. They need a college degree. They often have a higher degree called a PhD, or doctorate. They work in laboratories where they use microscopes. They also work in some amusement parks where there are water world attractions. Marine Biologists are also needed on fish farms where fish are grown for us to eat.

Circle the pictures that have something to do with marine biologists.

(answers on page 60)

QUESTIONS••••••••••••••••••••••••••••••

1. Where does a marine biologist work?

_____

2. What does a marine biologist study?

_____

3. What kind of education is needed to become a marine biologist?

_____

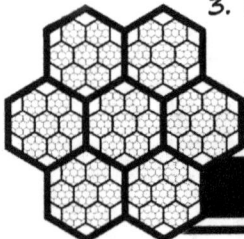
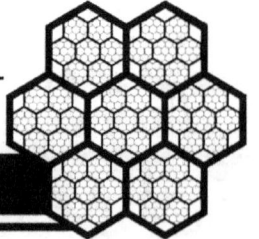

MARINE BIOLOGIST

Marine biologist ...that's for me.
I'll study life beneath the sea.
Check out turtles, fish and dolphins...
whales and plants and
ocean bottoms.

Write your own poem here

_____
_____
_____
_____

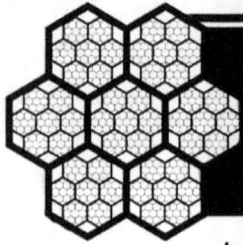
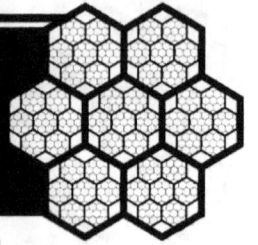

MILITARY
(mil'-i-tar-y)

In order to become part of the military a person must enlist, or join, the Army, Navy, Air Force, Marines, or Coast Guard. This means he or she agrees to serve our country. A high school diploma is required to join the military. The military serves around the world. The military services protect our country from enemies and helps other countries protect themselves. They use jeeps, ships, planes, helicopters, and tanks among other things.

Draw a line to match the officer to the branch of service.

AIR FORCE   ARMY   MARINE   NAVY   COAST GARD

Now name the different types of military transportation below.

_____   _____   _____   _____   _____

(answers on page 61)

QUESTIONS••••••••••••••••••••••••

1. How can a person become a part of the military?

_____

2. How much education does a person have to have to be in the military?

_____

3. What does the military do?

_____

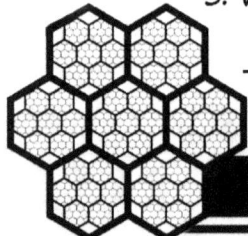
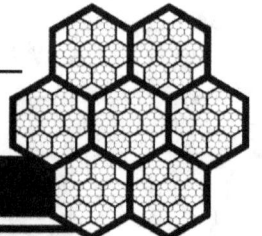

MILITARY

Army, Navy, Air Force, Marines,
Coast Guard Services too;
I want to serve, defend, protect.
Who wouldn't, wouldn't you?

Write your own poem here
_____
_____
_____
_____

NURSE

A nurse is someone who has a college education and is trained to provide medical care for sick, injured, or disabled people. Nurses also work with people who want to avoid becoming sick. They can be men or women. Nurses must have a license (which is legal permission to practice). They work in all areas where medical care is needed like hospitals, clinics, schools and doctors' offices.

Use the Clue Box to describe what these Nurses are doing

_____

_____

CLUE BOX

* caring for babies
* giving medicine
* taking care of children
* bandaging the wounded
* using a stethoscope to listen to the heart

_____

_____

_____

(answers on page 61)

QUESTIONS••••••••••••••••••••••••

1. Where do nurses work?

_____

2. Can nurses be men or women?

_____

3. How does someone become a nurse?

_____

4. Would you like to become a nurse? If so, why?

_____

NURSE

I want to be a nurse one day...
treat sick and injured too.
Give medicine and tender care.
Yes, that's what I will do.

Write your own poem here

_____

_____

_____

_____

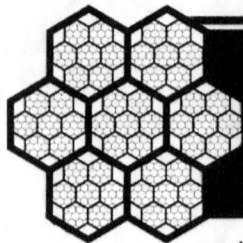
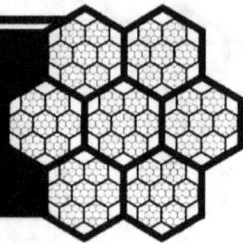

PHYSICAL THERAPIST

(phys'-i-cal ther'-a-pist)

A physical therapist is a health care professional who is licensed to treat illnesses or injuries by using activities and exercises that improve body functioning. Physical therapists have a college degree and a Ph.D., which is a doctorate degree. Some forms of treatment are massage, exercise, and heat therapy. Physical therapists sometimes visit patients in their homes. They also work in hospitals and clinics and rehabilitation centers. Rehabilitation centers are places with special equipment where people go to improve their ability to get around.

Use the Clue Box to describe these Physical Therapy activities.

CLUE BOX
* practice walking
* running
* lifting weights
* stretching exercises

QUESTIONS..........................

(answers on page 61)

1. Where do physical therapists work?

_____

2. How do they help people?

_____

3. How does someone become a physical therapist?

_____

4. What do physical therapists do?

_____

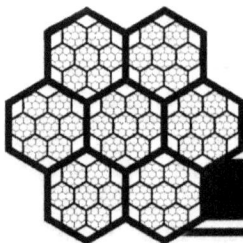
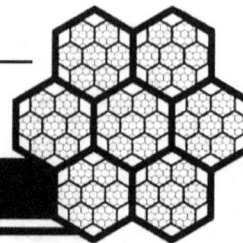

PHYSICAL THERAPIST

When you've been hurt or injured
and you don't know what to do...
Physical therapists will be there
to help you feel like new.

Write your own poem here

_____
_____
_____
_____

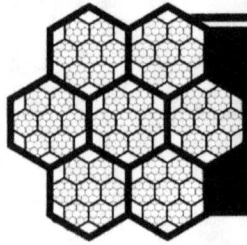
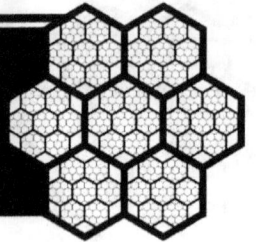

PILOT
(pi'-lot)

A pilot is someone who has been trained to fly all sorts of air crafts.
Some air crafts are commercial airplanes, helicopters, blimps, and more. Pilots must spend many hours learning and practicing flying planes. They need to attend aviation schools and/or take lessons in order to learn those skills. They need a pilot's license if they want to be a professional pilot.

Use the Clue Box to unscramble the words below.
They form the phrase that will answer the question
that is under the airplane.

CLUE BOX
* around
* world
* the
* Fly
* planes

What do Pilots like to do?

ylF   naples   ranoud   hte   rlowd

_____   _____   _____   _____   _____

(answers on page 61)

QUESTIONS ••••••••••••••••••••••••••••

1. Name some different kinds of airplanes?

_____

2. How does someone become a pilot?

_____

3. Would you like to become a pilot, and why?

_____

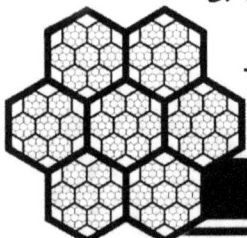
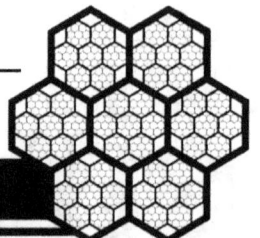

PILOT

Someday I'll be a pilot,
and soar above the clouds
in helicopters, jets and more ...
Now won't that make
me proud!

Write your own poem here

_____
_____
_____
_____

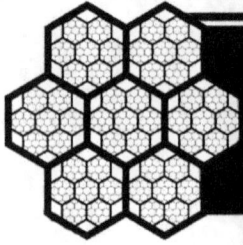

PLUMBER

(plumb'-er)

A plumber is someone who installs and repairs pipes and water lines in kitchens, bathrooms, heating, and irrigations systems. They learn their trade by being an apprentice and/or by attending a trade school. An apprentice is someone who learns a trade by working with a professional in that trade. Plumbers use wrenches, pipe cutters, drain cleaners, and other plumbers' tools in their job.

Plumbers work on many things. Use the Clue Box to name some of those things.

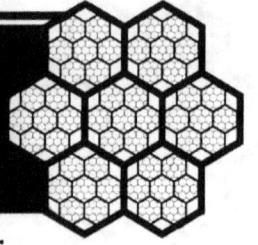

CLUE BOX

* pipes
* shower
* lawn sprinklers
* toilet
* hot watertank
* leaky faucet
* washing machine
* sink

_____ _____ _____ _____

_____ _____ _____ _____

(answers on page 62)

QUESTIONS••••••••••••••••••••••••••

1. How does someone become a plumber?

_____

2. What is an apprentice?

_____

3. What are some tools used by a plumber?

_____

4. Would you like to become a plumber, and why?

_____

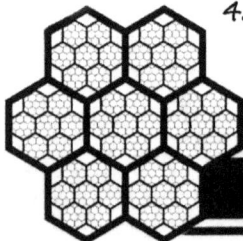

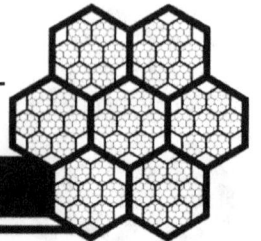

PLUMBER

Fixing pipes and water lines;
It really is no wonder. . .
that someday everyone you know
will need to call a plumber.

Write your own poem here

_____
_____
_____
_____

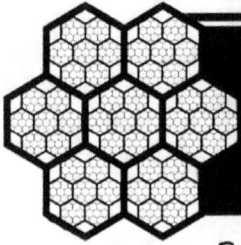

POLICE OFFICER

(po-lice' of'-fi-cer)

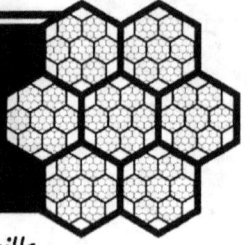

Police Officers attend academies (schools) where they learn the many skills needed to help the public, provide safety, and enforce the law. Men and women are police officers. They control traffic, give directions, help at accidents, and enforce the law by catching criminals. They work both day and night. They are our helpful friends when we are in need.

Use the Clue Box to describe the things that these police officers are doing.

CLUE BOX
* riding in police cars
* catching criminals
* controlling traffic
* giving tickets
* giving directions
* helping at accidents

_____   _____

_____ _____ _____ _____

QUESTIONS••••••••••••••••••••••••••••

(answers on page 62)

CIRCLE TRUE or FALSE

1. Police can be men or women. (True / False)
2. Police officers must be 7 feet tall. (True / False)
3. Police officers come to help. (True / False)
4. Police officers can run 100 miles per hour. (True / False)
5. Police officers sometimes can work all day or all night. (True / False)
6. Police officers can be your friend? (True / False)

7. Would you like to become a police officer, and why?_____

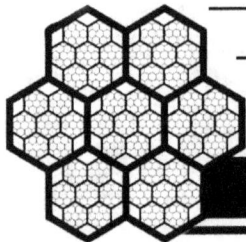

_____

_____

_____

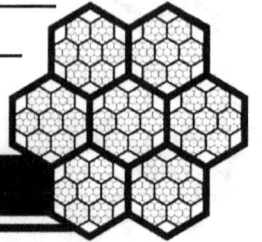

POLICE OFFICER

Police help us when we're in need ...
Fight crime, protect us too.
Enforce the law, maintain the peace.
So much for them to do.

Write your own poem here

_____

_____

_____

_____

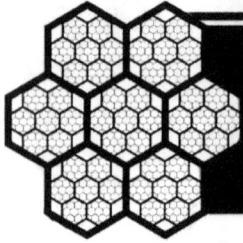

PROFESSOR
(pro-fes'-sor)

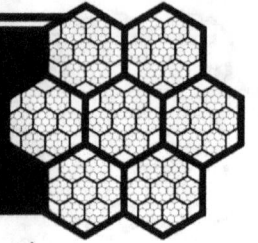

A professor is someone with a college education and advanced degrees such as a masters and a Ph.D. (doctorate degree). They have a special subject that they are certified to teach. Professors teach at institutions of higher learning such as colleges, universities, and specialty schools.

Draw a line from the picture to the word or phrase that relates to being a professor.

books   University/College   students/classroom   Laboratory   Computer

(answers on page 62)

QUESTIONS••••••••••••••••••••••••

1. What education does someone need in order to become a professor?

_____

2. Why are college professors sometimes called "Doctor"?

_____

3. Would you like to become a professor, and why?

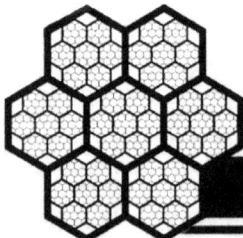

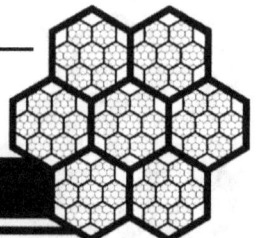

_____

PROFESSOR

Some careers need extra knowledge;
so some folks must go to college...
where professors can be found ...
to help and teach us
all year round.

Write your own poem here

_____
_____
_____
_____

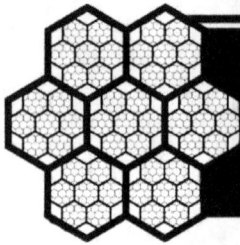
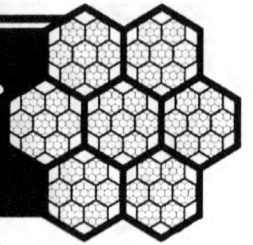

SPEECH THERAPIST
(speech ther'-a'-pist)

A speech therapist is someone who needs a college degree and a masters degree. A masters degree requires extra college courses. Speech therapists treat people with speech difficulties such as a stutter or a lisp. They know all about the mouth, tongue, throat, voice box (larynx) and anything involved in speaking. A stutter is when a person who has difficulty speaking without repeating sounds or words. A lisp is when a person has difficulty pronouncing the sounds (s) and (z). Speech therapists can help people develop new speech habits in order to overcome problems.

Use the Clue Box to unscramble the words below. Those words will answer the question.

CLUE BOX
* over
* talk
* it
* Let's

"What did the speech therapist say to the student who was shy and spoke with a lisp?"

teL's   aklt   ti   vreo

_____   _____   _____   _____

(answers on page 62)

QUESTIONS••••••••••••••••••••••••••••

1. How does someone become a speech therapist?

_____

2. What do speech therapists do?

_____

3. Would you like to become a speech therapist, and why?

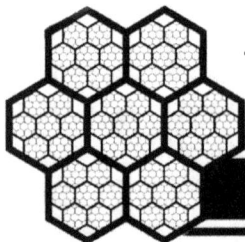
_____
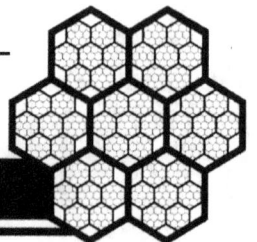

SPEECH THERAPIST

LAH, LAH, LAH
LAH, LAH, LAH
LAH, LAH, LAH
LAAAAAHH!

Some folks have a problem speaking
words that may be hard to say.
Speech therapists can help with that...
and I will too some day.

Write your own poem here

_____

_____

_____

_____

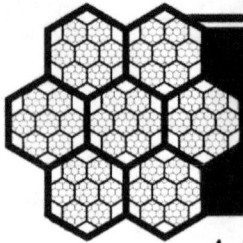
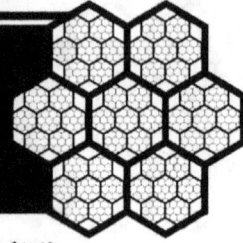

TEACHER
(teach'-er)

A teacher is someone with a college education who instructs people in many different areas. Most teachers have a specialty that they teach like math, science, history or physical education. They also teach specific age groups such as elementary or high schools.

Use the Clue Box to describe where teachers work.

CLUE BOX
* class room
* computer lab
* gym
* music room
* science lab

_____   _____

_____   _____   _____

(answers on page 63)

QUESTIONS••••••••••••••••••••••••

1. What are some different kinds of teachers?

_____

2. How does someone become a teacher?

_____

3. Would you like to become a teacher, and why?

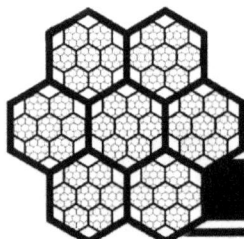
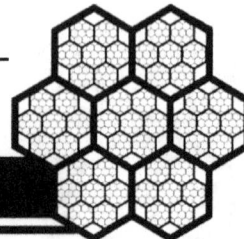

_____

TEACHER

I want to be a teacher....
to help children as they grow.
I want to show them how to learn
the things they need to know.

Write your own poem here

_____
_____
_____
_____

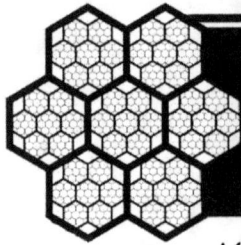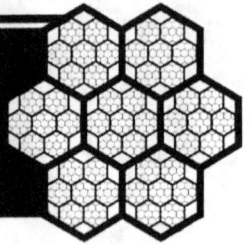

VETERINARIAN
(vet-er-i-nar'-i-an)

Veterinarians are doctors who treat animals. They specialize in either large animals such as farm or zoo animals, or small animals such as household pets. They must earn a college degree and then go to veterinary school to earn their DVM, Doctor of Veterinary Medicine. Veterinarians work in hospitals, clinics, farms, zoos, and wildlife preserves.

Circle the picture that have something to do with being a veterinarian.

(answers on page 63)

QUESTIONS••••••••••••••••••••••••

1. How does someone become a veterinarian?

    _____

2. Name some animals that veterinarians care for?

    _____

3. Where do veterinarians work?

    _____

4. Would you like to become a veterinarian, and why?

    _____

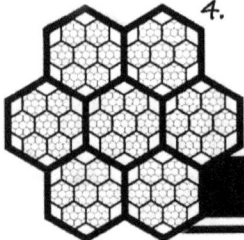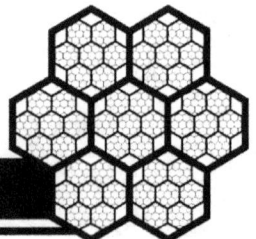

VETERINARIAN

I want to work with animals
like veterinarians do.
Make them well, heal their wounds.
Who wouldn't! Wouldn't you?

Write your own poem here
_____
_____
_____
_____

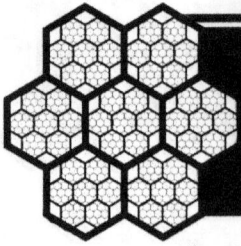
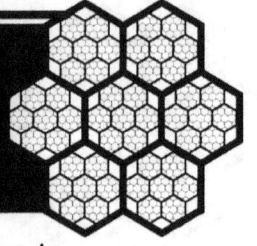

WRITER
(writ'-er)

A writer is someone who gets paid to write. There are many different ways to write such as fiction (make believe), non-fiction (true stories), and poetry (fancy writing that may rhyme). You can also write for newspapers and magazines or write biographies, songs, or plays. In order to become a writer you simply need to enjoy writing, do it often, and write about the things you like. From there, you then get the education needed to improve your writing.

Use the Clue Box to identify some different types of writing.

CLUE BOX
* books
* comics
* magazines
* newspapers
* stage plays
* movies
* TV Shows

_____   _____   _____

_____   _____   _____   _____

(answers on page 63)

QUESTIONS••••••••••••••••••••••••••

1. How does someone become a writer?

_____

2. What are some different types of writing?

_____

3. Would you like to become a writer, and why?

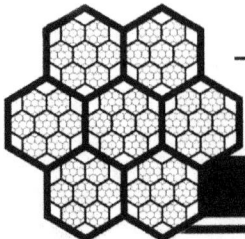
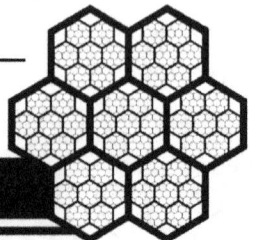

_____

WRITER

I love to write all kinds of things...
like poems, books and more.
When I grow up, I'll write about
the things that I adore.

Write your own poem here

_____
_____
_____
_____

COMPOSITION

Write a composition about what you would like to be when you grow up. Write about the things you'll do and how you'll do them. Write about how you'll get to where you want to go. Don't be afraid to change your mind. You'll find you have many interests, many skills, and many talents that you can apply to lots of different careers. So now that you have begun to explore, LET THE FUN BEGIN!

Be sure to include in your composition:
* Things you like to do.
* Things you are good at doing.
* What kind of work makes you happy.

Answer Key

ACCOUNTANT

CALCULATOR   DESK   BOOK   COMPUTER

QUESTIONS answers:
1. An accountant works with numbers and maintains the records of money that is spent and received by companies and private individuals.
2. Some accountant tools are desks, pencils, calculators, and numbers, numbers, numbers.
3. Accountants must go to college and take business courses.

ANTHROPOLOGIST

ARTIFACT   ARTWORK   EXAMINE   MUMMY TOMB   WORLD

1. An anthropologist studies mankind in the past and in present day. They examine ancient cultures.
2. Ancient cultures are groups of people who lived hundreads, or even thousands of years ago.
3. Artifacts are objects made by man.
4. A college education is needed to become an anthropologist.

ARCHITECT

ARCHITECT TOOLS   MEASURING TAPE   PYRAMIDS   BUILDINGS

1. Architects create plans for buildings, bridges, and other kinds of structures like the pyramids.
2. Some tools used by an architect are tape measures, desks, pencils, rulers, and calculators.
3. To become an architect, a college education is needed.

ASTRONAUT

SPACE SUIT   SPACESHIP   STARS   PLANETS

1. An astrononaut explores outer space and the planets.
2. Tools used by an astronaut are spaceships and space suits.
3. To become an astronaut a college education and studies in astrophysics are needed.
4. John Glenn was a famous astronaut.

AUDIOLOGIST

Unscramble Key: otoscope / ear / audiologist / audiometer

QUESTIONS answers:
1. An audiologist is an ear doctor who knows all about the ears and problems with hearing.
2. In order to become an audiologist, a college degree, and advanced degree called a PHD or doctorate, is needed.
3. Audiologists work in schools, hospitals, clinics, and private offices.

CARPENTER

| TOOLBOX | SAW | HAMMER | WRENCH | SCREWDRIVER |

1. A carpenter is someone who makes and repairs wooden objects such as chairs, tables, furniture, houses, and more.
2. Some tools used by carpenters are saws, hammers, nails, screwdrivers, and much more.
3. There are many ways to become a carpenter. One such way is to be an apprentice. An apprentice works and learns skills from someone who is a master carpenter.

CLERGY PERSON (CLERIC)

| CHURCH | SYNAGOGUE | MOSQUE | TEMPLE |

1. A clergy person takes care of the spiritual and religious needs of people.
2. Different kinds of clergy: Minister, Priest, Rabbi, Imam, and Monk
3. Clerics work in churches, synagogues, mosques, temples, and other houses of worships.

COMPUTER PROGRAMMER

CONNECT THE DOTS IS A PICTURE OF A COMPUTER AND KEYBOARD

1. A computer programmer designs programs for the operation of computers, They also test programs. They write codes that tell the computers what to do. They troubleshoot or "look for problems" and then solve the problems.
2. Computer Programmers usually work in offices.
3. A college degree and technical certification are needed to become a computer programmer.

Answer Key

DOCTOR

ELEMENTARY SCHOOL ----> HIGH SCHOOL -----> COLLEGE/MED SCHOOL ---> INTERNSHIP/HOSPITAL

QUESTIONS answers:

1. To become a doctor you have to graduate from college and medical school. Then you must complete an internship which is like an apprenticeship, where you have learned skills on the job.
2. Some different kinds of doctors are pediatricians, surgeons, general practitioners, and cardiologists.

EMERGENCY MEDICAL TECHNICIAN

AMBULANCE   SLING & BANDAGE   STETHOSCOPE   STRETCHER   GLOVES

1. EMTs take care of people who need immediate attention beacuse they are sick or injured.
2. EMTs travel in ambulances or emergency trucks that have medical equiptment inside.
3. EMTs go to schools for special training in emergency care such as bandaging wounds, giving medicine, delivering babies, helping choking or drowning victims. They take care of people who suddenly become sick or injured and need to get to the hospital right away

---

FIREFIGHTER

WORDS THAT SHOULD BE CIRCLED:

HOSE HELMET HYDRANT WATER FLAMES BOOTS LADDER PICKAXE ALARM

1. Firefighters sleep in the firehouse when they are on duty and there is no fire, unless they are volunteer firefighters.
2. Volunteer firefighters are only on duty when a fire alarm is sounded. They come from home or work to the firehouse to join other firefighters, Many smaller towns have voluntary fire departments.
3. Firefighters put out fires and respond to accidents where a fire might start.
4. To become a firefighter you must attend and complete special schools that teach the skills needed and pass the tests that are required.

GEOLOGIST
PICTURES THAT SHOULD BE CIRCLED

1. Geologists work all over the world studying solids and liquids that make up earth. They also study how the earth became the way it is.
2. Geologist use all kinds of equipment; digging and measuring tools, and tools to measure soil, metals, and rocks.
3. Geologist need a college degree.

Answer Key

GUIDANCE COUNSELOR

CHOOSE THE RIGHT PATH

PROBLEM SOLVING

LEARN TO WORK TOGETHER

PREPARE FOR HIGHER EDUCATION

QUESTIONS answers:
1. A college degree is needed to become a guidance counselor.
2. Guidance counselors work in schools with students in all grade levels.

LAWYER

ELEMENTARY SCHOOL --->

HIGH SCHOOL --->

COLLEGE PRE-LAW --->

LAW SCHOOL --->

PASS THE BAR EXAM

2. Lawyers work in offices and courtrooms.
3. The Bar Exam is a test that must be taken and passed in order to become a lawyer. It tests a person's knowledge of the law.

LIBRARIAN
PICTURES THAT SHOULD BE CIRCLED

LIBRARIAN

COMPUTER

BOOKS

BOOKSHELF

1. Libraries are found in schools, offices, some companies and public library buildings.
2. In order to become a librarian, a college degree in library sciences is needed.
3. Librarians help with research, arrange special programs in the library, and find the right books for the right projects.

MARINE BIOLOGIST
PICTURES THAT SHOULD BE CIRCLED

1. Marine biologists work in oceans and seas, some water world parks and fish farms.
2. Marine biologists study all forms of life in oceans and seas.
3. A college education is needed to become a marine biologist.

Answer Key

MILITARY

COAST GUARD　ARMY　NAVY　MARINE　AIR FORCE　JEEP　TANK　HELICOPTOR　SHIP　JET

QUESTION answers:

1. To become part of the military you must enlist (join) the Army, Navy, Air Force, Marines, or Coast Guard.
2. A high school education is needed in order to enlist in the military.
3. The military protects our country from its enemies and helps other countries do the same.

NURSE

GIVING MEDICINE　　HELPING CHILDREN　　USING STETHOSCOPE　　CARING FOR BABIES　　BANDAGING WOUNDED

1. Nurses work in hospitals, clinics, schools, rehabilitation facilities, doctor's offices, insurance companies, private duty in the homes of patients, and any other place where a nurse is needed.
2. Yes, nurses can be men or women.
3. A college education is needed to become a nurse.

PHYSICAL THERAPIST
ACTIVITIES DESCRIPTION

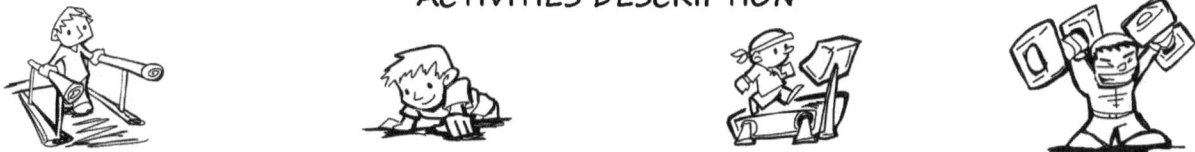

PRACTICE WALKING　　STRETCHING EXERCISING　　RUNNING　　LIFTING WEIGHTS

1. Physical therapists work in hospitals and rehabilitation facilities. Sometimes they also work in the homes of some patients.
2. They help people by working out a plan to improve their mobility (ability to get around) and helping people carry out that plan.
3. To become a physical therapist you must obtain a Doctorate Degree in Physical Therapy. That is an advanced degree after graduating from college.
4. Physical therapists help people with injuries or illnesses improve their ability to get around. They use exercise, massage, and heat therapy to help people feel better.

PILOT

UNSCRAMBLE THE WORDS

(ylF) FLY　　(naples) PLANES　　(ranoud) AROUND　　(het) THE　　(rldwo) WORLD

Answer to Question: Fly planes around the world.

1. Some different kinds of planes – commercial, passenger, jets, helicopter, and blimps.
2. To become a professional pilot you must take many hours of flying lessons and possibly attend an aviator college.

Answer Key

PLUMBER

| DRIPPING FAUCET | LAWN SPRINKLERS | PIPES | HOT WATER HEATER | SINK | SHOWER | TOILET | WASHING MACHINE |

QUESTION answers:
1. In order to become a plumber, you can attend a trade school or work as an apprentice with a professional plumber. An apprentice is someone who works with a professional in order to learn a trade
2. Some tools used by plumbers are wrenches, pipe cutters, drain cleaners, and pipes.

POLICE OFFICER

| CONTROLLING TRAFFIC | CHASING CRIMINALS | WRITING TICKETS | GIVING DIRECTIONS | HELPING WITH ACCIDENTS | RIDING IN POLICE CARS |

TRUE/FALSE ANSWERS: 1. TRUE   2. FALSE   3. TRUE   4. FALSE   5. TRUE   6. TRUE

PROFESSOR

| STUDENTS/CLASSROOM | COMPUTERS | BOOKS | LABORATORIES | UNIVERSITY/COLLEGE |

1. To become a professor you need a college degree, plus one or more advanced degrees, such as a masters and usually a PhD.
2. Professors who have earned a PhD are called doctor because the PhD is a doctorate degree.

SPEECH THERAPIST

UNSCRAMBLE THE WORDS

(teL's) LET'S   (aklt) TALK   (ti) IT   (vreo) OVER

Answer to Question: LET'S TALK IT OVER.

1. A lisp is when a person has difficulty pronouncing the sound of the letters "S" and "Z".
2. A college degree and a masters degree are needed to become a speech therapist.
3. Speech therapists help people who have problems with their speech, pronouncing some words, or communications.
4. Speech therapists work in schools, hospitals, rehabilitation facilities, colleges, and private practices.

TEACHER

COMPUTER LABS   MUSIC ROOM   CLASSROOMS   SCIENCE LABS   GYMS

QUESTIONS ANSWERED:

1. Different kinds of teachers – high school and elementary schools. There are teachers for all subjects, such as English, music, art, math, history, physical education, and all other subjects taught in school.

2. To become a teacher you must get a college degree in the area you want to teach.

VETERINARIAN

PICTURES THAT SHOULD BE CIRCLED

1. To become a veterinarian you must go to college and take science courses related to medicine, such as biology. Then attend a veterinary college for at least 3 years to become a doctor.

2. Some animals that veterinarians care for are dogs, monkeys, birds, cats, horses, gerbils, cows, pigs, lions, tigers, bears, and just about any animal on earth.

3. Veterinarians work in animal hospitals and clinics, farms, zoos, wildlife preserves, and anywhere there are animals.

WRITER

MAGAZINES   TV SHOWS   NEWSPAPERS   COMIC BOOKS   BOOKS   MOVIES   PLAYS

1. To become a writer you should write every chance you get and take classes to help you learn how to write well.

2. Different types of writing are books, comics, magazines, newspapers, movies, stage plays, tv shows.

I Wanna Bee

Here are some other Professions for you to consider:

- Artist
- Athlete
- Bookkeeper
- Bus Driver
- Chef
- CPA (Certified Public Accountant)
- Cartoonist

- Dancer
- Editor
- Graphic Artist
- Mortician
- Pharmacist
- Publisher
- Politician
- Secretary

Phillis Jones, RN

P.O. Box 2794 • Chesapeake, VA 23327